THIS IS CHARLESTON

THIS IS
CHARLESTON

A SURVEY OF THE ARCHITECTURAL HERITAGE OF
A UNIQUE AMERICAN CITY

Text By

SAMUEL GAILLARD STONEY

PUBLISHED BY THE CAROLINA ART ASSOCIATION,
CHARLESTON, SOUTH CAROLINA

First Published and Copyrighted in 1944 by

THE CAROLINA ART ASSOCIATION

135 Meeting Street

Charleston, S. C. 29401

Second Edition, 1960

Third Edition, 1964

Fourth Edition, 1970

Revised Edition, Copyright 1976 by the Carolina Art Association

Reprinted 1984

Printed in the United States of America

ISBN 910326-04-5

FOREWORD

"ᖴORTUNATELY, the past never completely dies for man. Man may forget it, but he always preserves it within him. For, take him at any epoch, and he is the product, the epitome, of all the earlier epochs. Let him look into his own soul, and he can find and distinguish these different epochs by what each of them has left within him."

Fustel de Coulanges
The Ancient City

No Charlestonian can be expected to speak or write about his city objectively for it is so much a part of the background of his mind and emotions that detachment is never possible. The lovely and the shabby are all woven into the same warp and woof of the familiar scene. The stucco façade of some old house, its chalky colors weather-faded, its surface mapped with earthquake patches and crumbling at the windows, through a sort of empathy assumes a character akin to an aged face looming out of one of Rembrandt's later portraits, infinitely world-weary yet infinitely enduring and wise in human experience.

New buildings do not have this quality and seldom acquire it in the lifetime of their builders, and those of shoddy construction without basic integrity achieve this distinction not at all, and do not deserve our veneration simply because of age.

It is generally conceded among architects that with the lapse of every ten years there is an appreciable change in the style and manner of building. This change was undoubtedly slower, and is today less easily detected, in the products of the 18th Century when society was more static, than later when change became accelerated. It is conceivable that a detailed study of what has come down to us until the present would disclose at least a score of perceptibly differentiated periods. Of course, the earlier buildings with the unmistakable cachet of the 18th Century will always surpass all others in their quality of workmanship, but with the early 19th Century came a greater variety and invention in planning and in the forms of enclosed space. By the middle of the last century there were many transient fashions adopted too lightly and inadvisedly, which tended to supplant the well-tried reasonableness of long-established craft customs. High ceilings, for example, were believed to induce coolness but they also multiplied the number of steps to climb, and stairways became vertiginous with the foothold narrow and precipitous as the flight swung through a quarter turn at the top, something that not even a journeyman carpenter would have considered workmanlike in the previous century.

By and large Charlestonians have reverted since World War One to what is generally believed to be "Colonial", sometimes descending to the meretricious, variety and as often as not flavored with extraneous elements borrowed from Williamsburg, Cape Cod, or stock millwork. While not entirely satisfactory to the fastidious, the general effect is not inharmonious in its setting.

What of the future? Without claiming to possess the gift of prophecy, there are certain facts clearly discernible before us.

The section headed "The Boroughs of Charleston" at the back of this book explains how from the earliest times private ownership of all the land north of Beaufain Street and its subsequent development as separate boroughs precluded the achievement of any comprehensive plan for the growth of the city. Today this lack of a workable plan has become more obvious with the lapse of time.

With three bridges across the Ashley River and a second bridge now being built across the Cooper, a west-east National Defense super-highway to terminate at Charleston, and another north-south artery to pass nearby are all factors which intensify the already acute traffic problems arising from the crazy quilt pattern of streets inherited from unguided private enterprise of ante-bellum days. Fortunately, the rerouting of streets south of the city limits can be accomplished without the sacrifice of any buildings of major interest. But comprehensive planning should not be postponed indefinitely.

The will to preserve our architectural heritage is as firmly rooted in the minds of our fellow citizens, as well organized and as rationally implemented as anywhere in this country. For this we have reason to be thankful for the civic consciousness and enduring efforts of many persons for many years.

In our justifiable preoccupation in preserving worthy survivals from the past, we have to some extent excluded the immediacy of the present and of the imminent future. Many worthy Charlestonians, whose motives are above question, view with alarm the erections on our sacred soil of any building designed in the contemporary manner. This does not follow, however, the traditions of our forefathers whose architecture was fully abreast of that of the rest of the country and often in the forefront, but always tempered by climate, custom and local preference.

After a couple of generations of experimentation and controversy, modern architecture has achieved orthodoxy throughout the civilized world although it has given rise to a great variety of sectarians. With its establishment it has naturally grown more conservative and responsible. It will in time grow more gracious, more urbane and more attuned to human emotions, and Charlestonians should prepare themselves for its acceptance but on their own terms. We should ask of our architects that our buildings be not only of our time but of our place. If we do this we can hope for another age of distinguished Charleston architecture.

ALBERT SIMONS, F.A.I.A. 1964

This is Charleston was the first inventory ever published of the historic architecture of an American city. Its importance in this respect is acknowledged in the introduction to the Historic Architecture Inventory which was completed in 1974 for the City of Charleston. Consultants for this recent project were Carl Feiss, internationally known planner; Russell Wright, eminent architectural historian; and Robert Anderson, city planning and architectural associate of Chapel Hill, N. C. They said about *This is Charleston*:

"The historic effect of *This is Charleston* is still to be fully documented. Without exception, though, its national influence as a first example of a comprehensive historic architectural study has been extraordinary. It set the stage for a number of neighborhood projects and updated variants. It certainly was basic to the National Register of Historic Places, begun in 1968 by the U. S. Department of the Interior.

"Those who put *This is Charleston* together were without question the most expert team on Charleston architecture which could be assembled, not only locally but nationally. Their work stands as a superb record and a challenge to today's efforts."

The expert team consisted of a group of Charlestonians who, foreseeing a new era for the city, determined to study the values of its past in order better to reconcile them with the necessities of the future.

They formed a committee under the leadership of the late Robert N.S. Whitelaw, the nationally known builder of miniature historical dioramas, who was then Director of the Carolina Art Association.

The Committee solicited and received grants from the Carnegie Corporation of New York and from the Rockefeller Foundation. They began work by taking the advice of Frederick Law Olmstead, city planner of Boston, whose urgent recommendation was that a very exhaustive stocktaking of Charleston's architecture be made.

Much of the work was accomplished in 15 months of 1940-41 by the committee's secretary, the late Helen Gardner McCormack, who made written and photographic reports on 1,168 buildings. Miss McCormack had been director of the Valentine Museum in Richmond, Va, and was to become director of the Carolina Art Association.

Buildings were classified by the following judges:

JOHN MEAD HOWELLS—Fellow of the American Institute of Architects, and author of *Lost Examples of Colonial Architecture* and other books.

ALBERT SIMONS—Associate National Academy of Design, Fellow of the American Institute of Architects, and editor with Samuel Lapham, Jr., of *The Early Architecture of Charleston (Octagon Library)* and *Plantations of the Carolina Low Country.*

ALICE R. HUGER SMITH—artist and author with D. E. Huger Smith of *The Dwelling Houses of Charleston,* illustrator of *A Carolina Rice Plantation of the Fifties,* and editor of *A Charleston Sketchbook by Charles Fraser.*

SAMUEL GAILLARD STONEY—B.S. in Architecture, author of *Plantations of the Carolina Low Country* and *Charleston: Azaleas and Old Bricks,* and other books.

Buildings were divided as to architectural value into five groups:

Nationally Important
Valuable to City
Valuable
Notable
Worthy of Mention

The first four of these classifications are illustrated with 572 photographs, listed by streets in alphabetical order. Where exact dates were not available, the age of the buildings is indicated by the following captions:

Pre-Revolutionary—before 1783
Post-Revolutionary—1783-1812
Ante-Bellum—1812-1860
Modern—1861-1944

This is Charleston was first published in 1944 by the Carolina Art Association. In 1960, when the original edition of 11,000 copies had been sold, the Association undertook a new edition, with the financial and editorial participation of two outstanding organizations working in this field: Historic Charleston Foundation and The Preservation Society of Charleston.

In subsequent editions, including this one, buildings that have been destroyed or mutilated since the 1944 edition are indicated by captions under the photographs; some fifty of the 572 originally pictured are now lost forever. New photographs have been substituted in some cases to show restoration work and to make buildings more recognizable.

With the aid of new research, more definite dates and new information have been added. Samuel Gaillard Stoney made minor changes in his text in 1960; otherwise it stands as written in 1944, with new information based on recent research added in an Editor's Note at the end.

March, 1976

THE PHOTOGRAPHS ARE ARRANGED ALPHABETICALLY
BY STREET AND IN NUMERICAL SEQUENCE.
ALL BUILDINGS CLASSIFIED IN THE SURVEY ARE LISTED
AT THE END OF THE PHOTOGRAPH SECTION.

THIS IS CHARLESTON

NYONE who knows the history of Charleston in the last few decades does not have to be told that her history, as vividly illustrated by her buildings, is not only one of her greatest assets, the living record of a wide and solid industry and culture, but also that it is a thing of value to the nation and, as such, a responsibility to the city.

Of all the older Atlantic seaports, Charleston, more than any other, has kept for us more buildings from more important periods of American history. So the town has become a place of pilgrimage to the rest of the country, and not only for that vast part of the country that grew westward from it and its sister cities, but for those sister cities themselves, which for reasons good or bad, have lost the heritage that we have kept. The result has been both flattering and profitable to Charleston. It has made her acquainted with a great many pleasant people who have grown to love her and have come here to spend their money. It is, therefore, an attribute that must be respected even when it is not appreciated.

Should you care to question the commercial value of Charleston's historical architecture, consider the history of Williamsburg. There, by means of an excellent job of archeology, an almost vanished provincial capital was resurrected in large part literally out of the ground. It

2 Amherst Street
c. 1802. Valuable

Camden Depot, Ann Street
Ante Bellum. Notable

South Carolina Railroad Warehouse
40 Ann Street. Ante Bellum. Notable

30 Anson Street. Ante Bellum
Notable, with notable garden
Garden GONE

2

St. Stephen's Episcopal Church
67 Anson Street
c. 1835. Valuable to City

79 Anson Street
After 1760. Valuable

71 Anson Street
c. 1806. Valuable

116, 114 Anson Street
Notable
GONE

75 Anson Street
c. 1800-c. 1838. Valuable

Unitarian Church, 6 Archdale Street
1852. Valuable to City

was a notable and lovely achievement. It has turned a sleepy Virginia village into a place of pilgrimage. It gives happiness to thousands and work to hundreds. Williamsburg, as provincial capital of the plantation colony of Virginia, had a fair share in making this nation. But Charleston was not only the capital of the Province of Carolina, but also its "mother-settlement," its seaport and town of trade, the heart and soul of the pioneer settlement of all the Southeast. Charleston has more historic architecture now than Williamsburg ever had even when it was truly new. For Charleston has not only kept buildings from the time of Williamsburg's brief prominence, but shows us, in house after house and street after street, pictures of its own life through the two long centuries of prosperity and culture. These are things which we should not lightly lose; but, unless we look out for them, they can vanish little by little through thoughtlessness, ignorance or want of a little care until this city becomes just another hum-drum version of the eastern seaport town.

It was to help guard Charleston from such a needless calamity that this book has been published. For in her case, the new age that has opened upon her with this war need not despise or destroy a great deal that she now can boast of. But the town is full of new blood, of people who do not know Charleston, and however they may appreciate the city's future, can hardly recognize or respect what she has kept from her past unless they are given some

St. John's Lutheran Church
10 Archdale Street
1815-18. Valuable to City

19 Archdale Street
Philip Porcher House
c. 1765. Valuable to City

21 Archdale Street
Dr. Samuel Wilson House
c. 1808. Valuable

4

23 Archdale Street
c. 1808. Valuable

38 Archdale Street
1797. Notable
GONE

41 Archdale Street
Old Fire Engine House
c. 1853. Notable
GONE

61 Ashley Avenue
Valuable

61 Ashley Avenue, gate and stable

70 Ashley Avenue
Ante Bellum. Notable

75 Ashley Avenue
Notable. Note doorway

knowledge of that past and the virtue of the landmarks it has left. As a graphic way of serving to supply a means to that end, these photographs are now published.

It should be fully understood that these photographs are only memoranda to you who see them, not works of art or even works of expert photography. What is hoped of them is that anyone, with this book in hand, may see this city through the eyes of a group of disinterested people who would like to point out to every Charlestonian, old or new, the buildings of all sorts that they have found valuable to their community.

It is hoped that this book will be used by you as a running reference, or rather, a walking one. Take it some day and go along the street you live on and see what houses and buildings it would have you look at. And we say advisedly the street you live on, because in making the survey the committee was more than ever impressed by the wide distribution of excellent and interesting buildings throughout Charleston. There are hardly any of our present day wards and none of our historical subdivisions that haven't either buildings or localities of considerable interest, historically or architecturally, or both.

As became the project of an art association, the committee concerned itself more with the actual qualities of the buildings it handled, than with their historical or sentimental values. But Charleston, by fulfilling her destiny as a true city, even when she had the proportions and the popula-

76 Ashley Avenue
1860. Notable

96 Ashley Avenue
Ante Bellum. Notable

107 Ashley Avenue
c. 1845. Valuable

6

113 Ashley Avenue
Valuable
Birthplace of Paul Hamilton Hayne

Porter Military Academy
167 Ashley Avenue
1844. Valuable to City
Old U. S. Arsenal
GONE

139 Ashley Avenue
Ante Bellum. Notable
Note terra cotta ornaments

178 Ashley Avenue
c. 1850. Valuable
Outstanding Greek Revival

163 Ashley Avenue
c. 1853. Notable
GONE

192 Ashley Avenue
Ante Bellum
Notable house, garden and stable
ALTERED

tion of a village, built usually with such dignity and individuality that history, sentiment and architecture came down to us hand in hand. So, therefore, by simply indicating a building that is worthy in itself of preservation, the survey often does a double duty by helping also to mark an historical or romantic subject. If you use these photographs properly, you will find that however they fail otherwise, they help to tell the story of Charleston as no words could; and that, after all, is what illustrations are supposed to do.

217 Ashley Avenue
Ante Bellum. Notable

Church of the Holy Communion
218 Ashley Avenue
1854-55. Valuable to City

1 Atlantic Street
After 1830. Valuable

3 Atlantic Street
After 1830. Valuable

8

8 Atlantic Street
Valuable

631 (East) Bay Street
Faber House
1838. Valuable

727 (East) Bay Street
Ante Bellum. Notable
Piazzas removed

56 Beaufain Street
Pre-Revolutionary. Notable
GONE

63, 65 Beaufain Street
Notable
Incorporated in Robert Mills Manor

Calvary Episcopal Church
71 Beaufain Street. Valuable to City
Built in 1847 for colored communicants
by the Episcopal Diocese
Now incorporated in Robert Mills Manor
GONE

CHARLESTON came into existence not only through a most royal gift and with a royal name, but in a right royal situation. The colony that the Lords Proprietors of Carolina sent from England to make a bridge-head on the shore of their Province, through the advice of the clever Cassique, or Chief, of the Kiawah Indians, established their initial settlement on this harbor in the spring of 1670. They did not guess then that they had picked upon the finest port in all the hundreds of miles of Atlantic coast King Charles II had included in Carolina. But almost at once they realized that the big peninsula lying between the rivers they soon named Ashley and Cooper was a most excellent site for a "town of trade and refuge" for their colony. So even while they were building up the first small temporary Charles Town on the south bank of the Ashley, they began to plan for a bigger and better one across the river on what they called White or Oyster Point.

For it six hundred acres were ordered reserved. But by neglect, or worse, by 1672 most of this had been granted away. Then a little more than three hundred acres were secured, and this was later surveyed for the "Grand Modell" that for the most part of a century guided Charleston's growing. This Grand Modell covered White Point up to a line from river to river, a part of which you will find still preserved by Beaufain Street. Below this boundary the dry lands on the point were laid off in streets and lots. Under order from

89 Beaufain Street
Post Revolutionary. Valuable to City
c. 1815

91 Beaufain Street, accessory building
Ante Bellum. Notable
GONE

102 Beaufain Street
Notable. Note Greek Revival detail
GONE

108 Beaufain Street, accessory building

32 Bee Street
Valuable
GONE

108 Beaufain Street
c. 1840. Notable

1 Broad Street
1853-1868. Valuable

5 Bedon's Alley
c. 1783-1790. Valuable
IMPROVED

12, 10, 8, 6 Broad Street
Notable
6, 8, 10, **GONE**

Anthony Ashley-Cooper, the most active and able of the Proprietors, these streets were made amply wide according to the best ideas of the time. These lines and the boundaries of the lots were laid down also with a fair degree of regularity. But White Point like all the lands along our tidal rivers was deeply and frequently penetrated by salt-creeks running through wide, almost bottomless, marshes. And these must have seemed nearly permanent obstacles to the first of Charleston's planners, for in several sections the property lines were fitted to the banks of creeks or rivers rather than to the axes of the principal streets. So trouble was laid up for the future. Some of these streams gave their bearings to future streets like Water Street which covers the buried bed of Vander Horst Creek. And the courses of two others made New and Savage Street diverge diagonally from the lines of all their neighbors. An active fault in the Grand Modell was also to make difficulties. Its squares between the streets were far too large. So as the city grew, private enterprise was allowed to cut niggardly passages through or into them and leave us such picturesquely inconvenient thoroughfares as Orange and Green-hill Streets, or the multitudes of alleys that have so often become little slums.

On the whole, the first governors of Charles Town had a very proper notion of the future needs of their town, Already by 1672, however, they had to contend with private inter-ests. John and Affra Coming, and

14 Broad Street
1799, facade **GONE**
Notable. Remodeled

15 Broad Street
Ante Bellum. Notable

South Carolina National Bank
16 Broad Street
1817. Valuable to City
Second Bank of U. S.

30, 28, 26 Broad Street
No. 28 Notable
30-1800; # 28-1791

49 Broad Street. Valuable
c. 1740. Restored 1963

33 Broad Street
Valuable. Note old office front
c. 1785

C & S Bank, Trust Dept., 50 Broad Street
Valuable. Formerly Charleston Library
Society. After 1796

35 Broad Street
Valuable

54 Broad Street
c. 1797. Notable
Fine office interior

Henry Hughes had been granted by then the larger part of the six hundred acre site on White Point. Enough of this was given back by Hughes to make up the three hundred odd acres taken by the Grand Modell. The rest, now lying between Beaufain and Calhoun Streets, as we shall see later, was to be cut up into boroughs and villages, and other small subdivisions, each with its own rather independent street system. You may see also what a set-back this was to the future town if you will count the streets that dead-end on Beaufain Street today and figure the trouble that such lack of continuity means to the city.

Confederate Home, 60-64 Broad Street
Valuable. Formerly Carolina Hotel
Courtyard very interesting

On White Point, the best region for business was the earliest built upon. Along the Cooper, between Vander Horst Creek and another water-course buried now under the Markets, was a stretch of bluffish, marsh-free, river bank that lent itself readily to wharf building. Along its edge, a "Bay," or wide street, was run where part of East Bay is to-day, and behind it the commerce of the growing port began to build a city.

For Charles Town was, in spirit at least, already something of a city when in 1680 the government of the Province moved across the Ashley to White Point. By then, or soon thereafter, Charlestonians of those days discovered a number of advantageous things concerning their country. Every year they drove an Indian trade for peltries and deer skins further back into the country, until by 1700 it extended beyond

67 Broad Street
Notable

68 Broad Street, Daniel Ravenel House
c. 1796. Valuable.

14

City Hall, 80 Broad Street
1801. Nationally Important

92 Broad Street
1740. Valuable to City. Home of
Dr. David Ramsay, the historian

85, 87 Broad Street
Valuable. Remodeled
1796

93 Broad Street
Post Revolutionary. Notable
1797

88 Broad Street
Post Revolutionary. Valuable
1813

95 Broad Street
c. 1770 Notable

the Mississippi. Already they were sending timber and provisions to the sugar islands; and they were on the verge of making rice a great staple crop that would give food, business, and sometimes riches to the people of Charleston for seven generations to come.

Also these pristine Charlestonians began to find out the superiority of their harbor. Both in itself and because of its position it was excellent. Nothing of the sort near it was so very fit for use by sea-going vessels. The shallow tidal streams that lace this coast and now are consolidated into the Inland Waterway had long since served as a protected passage for the dugouts of the Indians and the pettiaugers of the Spanish. By it small boats could pass along hundreds of miles of coast hardly anywhere risking the dangers of the open sea. Soon the "haul-overs" near Charles Town were open by cuts, and these streams became the freight-ways between the river and the island landings and the wharves along the city's bay. For these reasons Charleston became and remained the commercial center of the province as well as its capital. At the entry of the next century, she proved herself also very truly its city of refuge, and by this last function was notably modified in her growth.

In the opinion of the Spanish the whole project was a trespass on territory they had long claimed and sometimes tried to use. From their presidio of San Augustin de la Florida they tried unsuccessfully to wipe out Charles Town in the first year of its

100 Broad Street
Notable
GONE

102 Broad Street
Notable 1844

105 Broad Street
Notable
c. 1774

106 Broad Street
Dr. John Lining House. Before 1715
Valuable to City. Restored by the
Preservation Society of Charleston
1961

116 Broad Street. John Rutledge House
Pre-Revolutionary. Altered 1850 Notable

110 Broad Street, Ralph Izard House
c. 1728. Valuable to City

119 Broad Street
c. 1803. Notable

114 Broad Street
Col. Thomas Pinckney, Jr. House
Started c. 1790, finished c. 1829
Valuable

Cathedral of St. John the Baptist
122 Broad Street
1888-1907. Valuable to City

life. They succeeded later in destroying the little Scotch settlement of Stuart's Town farther down the coast. In turn the Carolinians raided Florida and in 1702 burned the town of San Augustin. When, at the opening of the 18th Century, France, by swallowing up Spain, threw Europe into a great war, one of the minor objectives of the government of Louis XIV was the destruction of this colony. The Charlestonians expecting this compliment prepared for it. So when a French and Spanish fleet came to demand the surrender of Charles Town, they found it too well fortified to attack. The walls, bastions, moats and demi-lunes are all long since gone; but the space that they confined has never quite recovered from certain effects of them. Still that part of the city lying between Meeting Street and the Cooper, and Water and the Markets is often too thickly built upon for a semi-tropic town. Close building was then the European notion of town planning. The walls confirmed Charleston in this idea, and the exigencies of business continued it. The habit was a bad one for a semi-tropic city; primitive sanitation made it disastrous. By the middle of the nineteenth century the yellow fever epidemics, received by Charleston in part payment for her West Indian trade, found ready and regular focii of infection within the lines of the walled town. So a good part of it was given over to the dilapidations of a slum. In the last thirty years improvement in basic water-works, the lure of the antique, and the in-

180 Broad Street
Federal Officers' Prison
c. 1850. Notable

18 Bull Street, Blacklock House
1800. Nationally Important

48 Bull Street
Valuable. A plantation type house
ALTERED

18

96 Bull Street
Notable. Note cornice

112 Bull Street
Notable
GONE

99 Bull Street. Capt. Warrington
Dawson House. Notable. Altered

100 Bull Street
Notable

128 Bull Street
Thomas Grange Simons House
Before 1814. Notable

104 Bull Street
Notable

85 Calhoun Street
Valuable
Restored

nate virtues of the buildings in these debased areas began to bring them back to a more fitting use. But the scars of slumdom are still upon that region, as the ruins of Bedon's Alley and Philadelphia Street have born witness.

After the War of the Spanish Succession came that with the Yemmassee Indians. And, so far as this colony was concerned, this was the more deadly and important. Plantation regions as close as Goose Creek were all but harried out of existence, and the town swarmed with refugees from the country. One good, however, came of this trouble, for soon after we rid ourselves of the Yemmassees, we did the same by the Lords Proprietors, who by then had become only less objectionable in some ways than the Indians. The pause in development caused by these wars and politics marked the end of the first notable era in the growth of the city.

Charleston within herself shows little from this time, but in her immediate neighborhood on the plantations and among the country churches are notable examples of the architecture from this first era. Medway, Middleburg, Mulberry, the churches of St. James, Goose Creek, and St. Andrews, all bear authentic evidence to the growth of a spacious life. In the town the changes that came with growth, the improvements in building, both from better material and a better comprehension of the problems of life in this climate, destroyed and replaced where the disasters of the time did not.

Zion Presbyterian Church
123 Calhoun Street
1850. Notable
Built for colored communicants by the Presbyterians of Charleston
GONE

139, 141 Calhoun Street
Notable
GONE

Charleston Orphan House
160 Calhoun Street
1792. Remodeled 1855.
Valuable to City
GONE

20

207 Calhoun Street
Post Revolutionary. Valuable

Old Bethel Methodist Church. c. 1800
222 Calhoun Street. Valuable

214 Calhoun Street
Ante Bellum. Notable

261 Calhoun Street, Franke Home-
Lutheran Home for Aged
c. 1857. Notable
GONE

220 Calhoun Street
Dr. Benjamin Huger House. Notable

261 Calhoun Street
Accessory building.
GONE

From 1720 to the outbreak of the American Revolution, Charleston enjoyed long stretches of peace and prosperity that are still very well illustrated by surviving buildings. The protection of the British crown was so much stronger than the town's walls that she soon burst down those on her landward side and spread westward across White Point. By private enterprise some of the marshes that penetrated the peninsula were soon filled in, more or less carefully. Old streets were "continued" and new ones laid down upon these fills; but then, and long thereafter, conservative builders of the finer type of houses kept, wherever they could, to solider ground. And in this period of the Royal Government, this trait soon began to spot Charleston with curious little deposits of different styles of houses that seem to show no continuity of growth.

Toward the latter part of this time the town also began to grow to the north across the plantation that had been given back to Hughes and the Comings; but here in reversal of the legend of the Sybelline books, there were then seven owners where there had been two in 1672. So this "neck" plantation was now developed little by little through Rhettsbury, Ansonborough and Middlesex to the east of the Broad Path we now call King Street, and to the west of it, over the lands of the Wragg family, who owned what are now the blocks beside King Street, the Glebe lands given by Mrs. Affra Coming to the parish church of Charleston, the school lands north

268 Calhoun Street. c. 1838
Notable

274 Calhoun Street
c. 1802. Valuable

276 Calhoun Street
Kitchen building to number 274
Post Revolutionary. Modern doorways

22

Kinloch Home for Nurses
286 Calhoun Street
c. 1809. Valuable
Jonathan Lucas House

135 Cannon Street, "Islington Manor"
Post Revolutionary. Valuable
GONE

West Point Mill
West End of Calhoun Street
1860. Valuable to City
Reconstructed by the City and the
Works Progress Administration

6 Chalmers Street
Ante Bellum. Notable

134 Cannon Street
Ante Bellum. Notable
GONE

8 Chalmers Street, Fire Engine House
Ante Bellum. Notable.
Altered

of them that include now the College and the three squares west, northwest, and north of it, and the Village of Harleston, that had descended from Mrs. Affra Coming to her nephew, and remained to be developed by his family. Anyone in a hurry who tries to pass east and west or north and south through these otherwise indistinguishable properties will still curse their boundaries and the disunity of city planning their individual developments have caused.

Somewhat unexpectedly we find the oldest traceable building in Charleston not inside the Grand Modell but on the little plantation of William Rhett that became Rhettsbury. His house, now number 54 Hasell Street, known to have existed before 1716, will in spite of renovations—one pre-Revolutionary, one in the 1820's and one in the last couple of years—give you a fair notion of how Charlestonians were building at that time.

As might be expected, the great body of architecture left by the first part of the time of the Royal Government is found within the lines of the walls, though those who look for it there must remember that this region suffered particularly from devastating conflagrations. The most notable houses that can be authentically traced are to be seen along the west side of Church Street. Between Tradd and Water Streets, Colonel Robert Brewton's house, now number 71 Church Street, is a landmark of this time in more ways than one. As it was known to have been built before 1733, it is definitely one of

17 Chalmers Street, The Pink House
Pre-Revolutionary. Valuable

29 Chalmers Street
Notable. After Confederate War home of Carolina Art Association School Remodeled by the German Friendly Society

36 Chalmers Street
c. 1840. Notable

24

28 Chapel Street
Elias Vanderhorst House
After 1832. Valuable
Upper piazza modern

Gas Works
East End of Charlotte Street
Ante Bellum. Notable

34 Chapel Street, Toomer House
c. 1829. Notable

16 Charlotte Street
Robert Martin House
Valuable to City
1834-40

36 Chapel Street
Notable. Plantation type house

20 Charlotte Street
Joseph Aiken House
1848. Valuable to City

the oldest houses within the Grand Modell and the city. It is also almost as interesting for being almost our earliest example of the Charleston "single house." It is interesting to notice in that immediate neighborhood how you can trace the persistence of this plan through nearly every notable style of architecture Charleston used thereafter. For thereabouts house after house, large and small, followed the lead of this earliest generation that built particularly to suit the climate of this region. Brewton's house, though close set against a southern neighbor, until a short time ago was even more characteristic in that it had a piazza along its southern side. Apparently piazzas were largely of a later growth, however. But the scheme of the house standing endways to the street, broad side to the south or southwest, and one room thick, so suited Charleston that even our shanty towns were built on similar lines.

The house to the south of Brewton's marks the other great type from this period, the "double house." These, if more spacious and in some ways more convenient, were considered somewhat less comfortable than their single rivals. Below these two houses, to the south of the Baptist Church, is another very old house of the type of William Rhett's and probably contemporary with it. Opposite it are three small wooden houses of the single house plan built well before the Revolution and excellent models still of the simpler sort of dwelling house from the time of

29 Charlotte Street
Ante Bellum. Notable
c. 1828

32 Charlotte Street
Ante Bellum. Valuable
1820-25

33 Charlotte Street
Notable
c. 1854

36 Charlotte Street, Ante Bellum
Notable. Altered
c. 1830-39

44 Charlotte Street
Ante Bellum. Notable
c. 1834

40 Charlotte Street
Ante Bellum. Notable
1831

12 Church Street
Notable c. 1810

43 Charlotte Street
Ante Bellum. Notable c. 1849

19 Church Street
Valuable

the Royal Government. If you will pass up Church Street, you will find in the block north of Tradd on either side of the Heyward House two other representative Charleston buildings. Both are composites of residences and business establishments. The more northerly of these, once a lively negro "alley" still keeps its old contemptuous nickname of "Cabbage Row," which Dubose Heyward transposed into "Catfish Row" when he transposed a simulacrum of the building to the water front to house "Porgy" in his celebrated novel. "Cabbage Row" is typically a tenement according to the usage of the time when it was built, a commercial venture on the part of an individual who might never have lived in it himself.

20 Church Street
c. 1809. Valuable

Church Street is peculiarly rich in history. However, it is only one of any number of such regions that you find all about Charleston illustrating various periods of history. As such they are now absolutely invaluable to the community and worth all the care that can be given to their preservation.

24, 22 Church Street
c. 1796. Notable

The War of the Austrian Succession rudely broke in two the long comfortable prosperity of the Royal Government in Charleston. However, by cutting off the best foreign markets for rice, the war forced the Low Country to find in indigo a new and soon extremely profitable staple. Afterward, this crop, with rice and the still extensive Indian trade, gave Charleston her golden age. You can measure the two divisions still from the institutions they have left. From

35 Church Street
c. 1770. Valuable to City

37 Church Street
George Matthews House
c. 1750. Valuable to City

45, 47 Church Street
Notable
No. 45 built by T. Young, 1769,
and known as 14 Water Street

38 Church Street
Post Revolutionary. Notable

55, 57 Church Street
No. 55 Notable
No. 57 **GONE**

39 Church Street
George Eveleigh House
c. 1743. Valuable to City

59 Church Street
c. 1735. Valuable to City

the earlier half of the Royal Government date most of our old friendly and beneficent societies; but, from its second half we have still such souvenirs of a direct attainment of culture as its orchestral organization, the St. Cecilia Society, the Charleston Library Society and the Charleston Museum. The extent of its culture is easily understood if you will look at some of its architectural remains. For men who built such churches as St. Michael's in which to worship and such houses as those of Miles Brewton on lower King Street and John Stuart on Tradd Street in which to reside, surely knew how to live with an ample and cultivated grace.

Charleston's golden age preceded the Revolution; something more than a silver one followed. No other time has left more thoroughly good and beautiful building. Charleston, and the state that had grown out of her, suffered brutally in the war but recovered rapidly. About 1790 a tide of prosperity rose to flood on to the War of 1812. Several economic sources swelled its flood. Rice moved to the rich river fields; cotton came first to replace indigo and then excel it. Mechanics boosted both crops by breaking the bottle-necks in their preparation with the pounding mill and the gin. If the Indian trade was vanishing, white men's settlements that were killing it now sent tobacco and cotton that more than replaced the peltries and deer skins of the savages. These were the crops that made the "wagon trade" of upper King Street. And this method of

60 Church Street
Pre-Revolutionary. Valuable to City
c. 1758

First Baptist Church
61 Church Street
1822. Nationally Important
Robert Mills architect

69 Church Street
1745. Nationally Important

30

71 Church Street
Col. Robert Brewton House
c. 1720 Nationally Important

77 Church Street
c. 1819. Valuable
Shop with residence above

75 Church Street, warehouse and
stable of No. 77. 1810-16
Notable

78 Church Street
Post Revolutionary. Notable

76 Church Street
Post Revolutionary. Notable

79 Church Street
Notable
c. 1718 and c. 1742

transportation was soon supplemented by the Santee Canal, obviating a dangerous passage below the mouth of the river and bringing freight from the state's principal rivers by way of the Cooper to the wharves of Charleston. Those wharves were busier than ever before. British trade regulations were gone, and the North had not yet invented the protective tariff. Charleston traded where and, largely, as she pleased. Spain's great colonies were breaking away from her and this city served them as a free port where they might barter produces for European goods. Much of the money made at this time still benefits the city; how much you may begin to guess if you will look for one sure sign of the time. The town borrowed from England at this time the beautiful and elegant style of the Adam brothers. When once you learn to recognize its graceful proportions, its light and classic decorations, and its sound structure, you will begin to realize how many hundreds of houses and business buildings in Charleston come from this happy period.

The fortifications of the Revolution crossed the peninsula of White Point a little above the northern line of the Comings' and Hughes' property. Now, a section of Charleston long after officially known as the "Neck" was loosely built upon. Business, marching up the old Broad Path that was then losing its identity to King Street, set up wagon yards and their accompanying shops as high as the neighborhood of Line

83, 85 Church Street
c. 1749. Valuable to City

86 Church Street
Post Revolutionary. Valuable to City

87 Church Street, Heyward House
c. 1770. Nationally Important
Restored by the Charleston Museum
and the Society for the Preservation
of Old Dwellings

89, 91 Church Street, Cabbage Row,
alias Catfish Row. Post Revolutionary
Valuable to City

94 Church Street
c. 1759. Valuable to City

90 Church Street
c. 1760. Valuable to City

100 Church Street
Post Revolutionary. Notable

St. Philip's Rectory
c. 1807. Valuable to City

102 Church Street, rear
Notable. Rebuilt

Street. Landowners laid out smart subdivisions, some of them with a sense of city planning that was largely lacked before and long after. For, when the Wraggs partitioned off the borough to which they gave their surname as a title and their Christian names to distinguish its streets, they had the civic decency to make two pleasant little parks for it. Wragg Square and Wragg Mall, set aside for the use of the public by the estate of John Wragg in the year 1801, have been surely among the happiest investments ever made by a Charlestonian. Southeast of Wraggborough, the Mazycks ran streets through the pasture where the Liberty Tree had shaded carousing patriots as they cooked up the Revolution. North of Wraggborough, Henry Laurens developed the Village of Hampstead on what counts hereabouts for a hill. This pleasantly overlooked the marshes of the Cooper, since covered by the Union Station and railroad yards and docks. Laurens, like John Wragg, left a mall, or park, in Hampstead that still does valiant service as a green space in a not too happy neighborhood.

West of King Street, corresponding lands, much intersected by creeks that may as truly have been said to drain out of the Ashley as into it, were also laid off in pleasant boroughs and villages. Elliott and Radcliffe Boroughs have only the identity of a few street names, and in the case of the latter, in that of the church of St. Paul's, Radcliffeborough. West of this borough was one that took its name from Daniel

103 Church Street
Post Revolutionary. Notable

116 Church Street
Valuable

121 Church Street
Notable

124, 122 Church Street
Notable. Corresponding half of
gable removed from No. 126

134 Church Street
Post Revolutionary. Notable

128 Church Street
Notable

Dock Street Theatre
135 Church Street
Ante Bellum. Valuable to City
Reconstructed from the ruins of the
Planters Hotel by the City and the
Works Progress Administration

131 Church Street
c. 1809. Valuable

French Protestant Huguenot Church
136 Church Street
1844-45. Valuable to City

Cannon. Above it was Islington, and beyond Islington, the village of Washington, whose name descended to the old race course, used later as a ground for the Exposition, and now hidden under the oaks, the azaleas, and the roses of Hampton Park.

These last properties were only scantily built upon when the War of 1812 rather abruptly closed what Charleston might best call her Adam period.

143, 145 Church Street
Pre-Revolutionary. Valuable to City
Doorways modern

How abruptly this happened is shown by the stumps of two steeples. Business in Charleston, particularly that of the wagon-yard trade, was then to a very fair extent in the hands of Scotch-Irishmen, either directly imported, or come in by way of the Up Country. To mark their success and their piety, these had built the monumental Second, or Flinn's, Presbyterian Church. When money grew hard, upon the coming of the war, their hearts changed also, so that no spire ever rose above the drum that was to hold it. The planters who summered about Radcliffeborough, whose subscriptions to the building of St. Paul's nicknamed it the Planters' Church, reacted similarly. And it was left to another age to cap their Palladian structure with four Gothic finials and their concomitants.

St. Philip's Episcopal Church
146 Church Street
1835. Nationally Important

As in the two previous wars, Charleston marked her growth up the White Point peninsula by a set of fortifications; and the line of these of 1812 still leave their name, and mark their approximate location by Line Street.

St. Philip's Old Parish House
154 Church Street
Valuable to City

181 Church Street
Ante Bellum. Notable

110, 106, 102 Coming Street
Ante Bellum. Notable
102, 106 **GONE**

St. Luke and St. Paul's Episcopal Church
126 Coming Street
1811-16. Valuable to City

10 Coming Street
Notable

69 Coming Street
Notable

Cordes Street
Ante Bellum. Notable
Altered

Charlestonians were very fortunate a few years ago when one of the Wraggborough houses became the property of the Museum. This house, designed by Gabriel Manigault for his brother, Joseph, is one of the finest built in the Adam style with the additional virtue of coming from the hands of Charleston's first notable native architect. Those who would like to study the period can here find it beautifully exemplified. Since the original rich, but quiet, colorings have been rediscovered and restored, you get an excellent idea of the way the house looked when it was a very smart addition to a new suburb. But you can also find the style worthily represented all about the city that stood within the "lines" of 1812.

Charleston never defended these earthworks. No enemy needed to besiege them to affect radically the city's prosperity and history, and the city came out of this war into a changing world. The North, discovering an unnatural use of the tariff, began the long economic struggles between the sections, with Charleston as a chief Southern center of opposition. The Mechanical age, that hereabouts loosed the cotton crop on its imperial march across the Southern states, now began to cut away from Charleston a good part of the territory that had always traded with her. The steamboat, however much it added to the city's prosperity, was soon giving to Savannah a great share of the business from the upper part of Georgia and the section of South Carolina convenient

4-2 Court House Square
Daniel Blake's Tenements
1760-72. Valuable to City

8 Court House Square
Notable. Altered

Powder Magazine, 21 Cumberland Street
c. 1713. Valuable to City

38

105 Drake Street
Enston-Melchers Residence
Ante Bellum. Notable
GONE

13 East Battery
William Ravenel House
1845. Valuable
Portico lost in earthquake

1 East Battery
Louis de Saussure House
c. 1850. Notable

21 East Battery
Edmonston-Alston House
c. 1828. Valuable to City

9 East Battery
Robert William Roper House
1838. Valuable

39 East Battery
c. 1810. Valuable to City

to the Savannah River. Savannah marks in her architecture the great success of this cut into Charleston's old territory, until the older city, calling in the fire-new steam-railroad as an ally, built the longest road then in the world. With this she recaptured for a time her old trading posts at the fords of the Savannah and watched with wicked satisfaction as the great houses the steamboat had built in her upstart rival turned into boarding houses.

Shriners' Temple, 40 East Battery
Missroon House
1789-95. Notable. Altered

Following this initial experiment with railroads, Charleston tried several times more to take or retake trading territories to the west; but after this first coup her reach unhappily ever exceeded her grasp. States carved from her old trading territories, cities growing up on the sites of Indian towns where her people had fought the Louisana French for business, were jealous of her, or too busy developing railroads of their own to wish to co-operate. Railroads of themselves were reorienting the country, but not to Charleston's advantage. And one she succeeded in building, by a combination of over-ambitious planning and divided councils, was run literally into the ground at Stump House Mountain. But at least she held the ocean traffic of her state; and whatever else failed her, the rice of the Low Country, the cotton of the Middle and Up Country and the highbred staple of the Sea Islands still poured across her wharves into the world.

In the age of eclectic architecture, when steam, through the printing

43 East Bay
c. 1755. Valuable to City

45 East Bay
c. 1850. Notable

47 East Bay
Valuable. Dates c. 1740 but has
undergone frequent alterations

57 East Bay
c. 1783. Valuable
Balcony from 28 Queen Street

51 East Bay
After 1818. Valuable to City

71 East Bay
Modern. Notable. Good alterations
have made an asset of a poor building

53, 55 East Bay
Post Revolutionary. Valuable

78 East Bay, Vanderhorst Row
1800. Valuable

press, poured ideas out upon America far faster than they could be digested, Charleston did a fair, but not inordinate, amount of building. The city keeps many spacious houses from the Transitional Period in the 1820's when architects worked somewhat timidly away from the Adam elegance into the Greek Revival. Around the Village of Harleston especially, you find such signs of this time as mantels where dancing nymphs and lion-drawn chariots have given way to sprays of acanthus and spread eagles. Possibly the most notable house left from this time is that which Governor Thomas Bennett built for himself on Lucas Street and that now houses nurses and interns of the Roper Hospital.

Gabriel Manigault, Charleston's first great amateur in architecture, worked in the Adam Period and style. His logical successor, Robert Mills, one of the first truly professional architects in America, began to serve his native city in the Transitional Period. The Fireproof Building and the First Baptist Church are parts of the very considerable body of work that this most able constructor and artist has left here. Mills, a student of Hoban and Jefferson, had a nation-wide reputation in his time and worked all along the eastern seaboard of the United States.

When the Greek Revival was at its height, one of Charleston's calamitous fires cleared a space for it. On this account, anyone who wants to study this particular style can find it thoroughly spread through

83 East Bay
Post Revolutionary. Valuable
Doorway modern

In a dozen years this line of valuable old houses (Nos. 83, 87, 89, 91, 93, 95, 97, 101, 103 and 107) was gradually changed from slums into a valuable and handsome addition to the city.

85 East Bay
c. 1784. Notable

87 East Bay
Post Revolutionary. Notable
Balcony modern

91 East Bay
Post Revolutionary. Notable

89 East Bay
c. 1780. Valuable to City

93 East Bay
c. 1780. Notable

90 East Bay
c. 1835. Notable

95 East Bay
c. 1740. Valuable to City

what had been Ansonborough. Society Street, Wentworth Street and Hasell Street are well lined with it; and such buildings as the Charleston Hotel, the Hasell Street Synagogue and the Baptist Church on Wentworth Street are notable examples. Charlestonians can point with pride, however, to their forbears' use of this style, for here the massive Doric reserved by the Greeks for religious and public buildings served Charleston only in the same fashion; and the lighter Corinthian and Ionic modes were saved for domestic decoration. In fact, Charleston seldom employed, except for public buildings, the tall porticos that were elsewhere in America first used freely at this time, porticos that afterward were considered "colonial" and the prime essential of a Southern mansion to this day in the movies and the popular imagination. It had its fair share of these, as the home of Joseph Aiken, now number 20 Charlotte Street, and the old Kerrison House, now number 138 Wentworth Street, very charmingly witness. Though it must be remembered of the former example that the tin capitals now on its columns are singularily unhappy substitutions for the water-leaf type that were there originally.

The more strictly classic revival overlapping the Greek one gave us a charming version of a Roman temple for the Market Hall. In this style, too, an Edisto cotton planter built the residence on Rutledge Avenue at Montague Street that seems to have anticipated many years ahead the

97 East Bay
c. 1740. Valuable

101 East Bay
c. 1740. Valuable to City
Garage doors and iron work modern

103 East Bay
c. 1787. Valuable
Garage and doorway modern

44

107 East Bay
Notable

Exchange and Custom House
122 East Bay, 1767-72
Nationally Important, in spite of
adverse alterations. Restored by
the Daughters of the American
Revolution and Historic Charleston
Foundation

120, 118, 116, 114 East Bay
Coates' Row. c. 1800
Valuable

131 East Bay
Notable
GONE

120 East Bay, Old French Coffee Shop
c. 1800. Valuable

137 East Bay
Ante Bellum. Notable
GONE

needs of the Free Library that it lately housed.

Charleston also showed a discriminating taste in her handling of the revived Gothic of this period. Scraps of detail in the style occur within a few residences; but outwardly and sizably it was kept for ecclesiastical buildings only. The Huguenot Church is probably the best known Gothic structure in Charleston, but should yield its place in some ways to St. Luke's Church on Charlotte Street, both in design and for historic interest.

St. Luke's, like its neighbor, Flinn's Church, is steepleless because of a war. The younger church bears both negative and positive signs that the Confederate War ended the era when it was being built. One of the effects was fortunate, for the mortar made to stucco its walls in imitation of stone work went into Confederate fortifications and instead we have honest, handsome brickwork.

Concerning the War between the States, Charleston is well aware that more than any other southern city she began—and also lost it. She paid well for these distinctions. In the first year of fighting, when her streets were full of drums and marchings and a blockading squadron loomed ominously across the harbor-bar, the last of her disastrous fires drove a wide destruction across her. Beginning nearly where the Grand Modell's boundary came to water on the Cooper, the fire of '61 ran southwest across the territory of the Grand Modell, until it burned itself out where Council Street then

First National Bank, 139 East Bay
Before 1849. Valuable
GONE

First National Bank, 139 East Bay
Kitchen building
Improved

141 East Bay
1853-59. Valuable. Old Farmers and Exchange Bank. Moorish eclecticism

162-154 East Bay
Notable. Greek Revival in commerce
154 **GONE**

U. S. Custom House, 200 East Bay
1853-79. Valuable

178 East Bay
Post Revolutionary. Valuable
Iron work is notable

217 East Bay
Ante Bellum. Valuable
Greek Revival
GONE

188-192 East Bay
Post Revolutionary
Notable as a group

301 East Bay
c. 1816. Valuable

reached the Ashley. Financially, the loss was enormous; architecturally, it was truly incalculable. No one can now say all that it destroyed. The contrast of the inferior buildings plainly marking its course with those that stand beside it only let us guess at what is gone. For this time there was no following Greek Revival worthily to replace the losses. Instead, in the bad day of Reconstruction and Mid-Victorianism, the "Burned District" slowly recovered itself, but so slowly that thirty years later small dairy herds still were pastured among its chimney-stumps and cellar-holes.

Two years after the fire the war itself struck Charleston. The Federals, fighting their way up the barrier islands, first shelled the lower part of the city from their Swamp Angel Battery behind Morris Island. However, the gun, working at extreme range, burst before it could cause much more than panic. But after Gregg and Wagner changed hands came a bombardment both extensive and intense. A dud in St. Luke's wall traveled farther than most; but thousands of livelier shells forced the evacuation of the greater part of the city below Calhoun Street. Few buildings in that region escaped more or less serious hurt in the five hundred and eighty seven days of continuous military operation against Charleston that was ended by her evacuation in '65.

The poverty that came with peace was not, from our point of view, entirely an evil. Much that was good in the architecture of Charleston,

321 East Bay
Before 1800. Valuable

329 East Bay
c. 1800. Valuable to City

332 East Bay
c. 1817. Valuable

333 East Bay
Post Revolutionary. Valuable
GONE

344 East Bay
Valuable
See also page 8. Bay Street
renamed East Bay Street since
1944. **GONE**

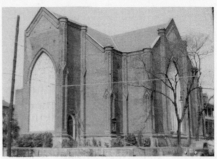

22 Elizabeth Street
Formerly St. Luke's Episcopal Church
Now Fourth Baptist Church
1859. Valuable to City

7 Elizabeth Street
c. 1843. Valuable
GONE

48 Elizabeth Street
Gov. William Aiken House
c. 1817. Valuable

19 Elizabeth Street
Ante Bellum. Notable c. 1841

16, 14 Elliott Street
Notable. A good restoration

which must have been doomed by prosperity in the tasteless '70's and '80's, survived of necessity to more sensible days. Outside the burned district, mansards, and what they cover and fit with, are mercifully few and far between. Even the "Queen Anne" successors to these "General Grant" hideousities and the "Colonial" of the early 1900's are fortunate rarities in the more interesting parts of the city.

As the city was beginning to recover from its second adventure in nation building, another disaster followed those of the war. Charleston, remembering her West Indian connections and her almost West Indian position, like the islands remembers also to look out for trouble in August. Hurricanes enough have come over her in that month, but in 1886 it was the earth that moved. A classic earthquake shook the city, destroying many old buildings and cracking almost every masonry wall. So much so that a pre-earthquake building is easily recognized by the great washers of the rods that bind its walls together.

It was fortunate for historic Charleston that the city's expansions at the beginning of this century worked their way first up the old "neck" and then covered the great fill of the Boulevard. A critical inspection of those two areas will show you how, at that time, American architecture was working its way back to decent ideas of design, but without local distinction. At the beginning of this period, Charleston, in an attempt to recapture her old trade with the

20 Elliott Street
c. 1793. Valuable

9 Franklin Street
Notable

13 Franklin Street
Ante Bellum. Notable

15 Franklin Street
c. 1850. Notable

4 Gadsden Street
Ante Bellum. Notable

17 Franklin Street
Ante Bellum. Notable

19 Gadsden Street
Ante Bellum. Notable

Old Marine Hospital
20 Franklin Street
1833. Nationally Important. Restored
as part of Robert Mills Manor and used
by the Housing Authority of the
City of Charleston
Robert Mills, architect

31 Gadsden Street
Ante Bellum. Notable.
GONE

West Indies, held an Exposition on grounds covered by and around the old Washington Race Course. With the end of the Exposition, the Race Course Grounds and the farms between them and the river were turned into Hampton Park and provided the city with her first big breathing space. Unfortunately no park was included in the planning of the Boulevard, but the long driveway along the Ashley more than makes up in many ways for this deficiency.

In the Boom prosperity after the first World War, the nation discovered Charleston. Until then, we had had a steady, but small, flow of discerning visitors for quite a long time. But the automobile and the cement highway flooded us every spring with admiring, if not always discerning, people. To a certain extent, these tourists forced Charleston to re-discover herself. By accentuating the value of the town's appearance and spending money in the process, the tourists woke up many citizens to values that they had never guessed at or rather resented.

From these influxes Charleston kept a number of valuable and interesting "winter" people, both within her limits and on the adjoining plantations. Many of them have proved invaluable to the land of their adoption. To offset this, in the Boom Days the town found it had to protect itself from collectors of everything from ironwork to complete houses. Some of these last were taken down and carried off completely, from the brickwork of the basement to the timber of the roof. To guard against

4 George Street
Ante Bellum. Notable

7, 9, 11 George Street
Ante Bellum. Notable as a group
No. 9 **GONE,** No. 11 **GONE**

Water Works, 14 George Street
c. 1797. Valuable to City
Middleton-Pinckney House

52

20 George Street
Ante Bellum. Notable **GONE**

21 George Street, Ripley House
c. 1840. Valuable **GONE**

28 George Street
Ante Bellum. Notable

30 George Street
Ante Bellum. Notable **GONE**

36 George Street
Ante Bellum. Valuable

72 George Street
Ante Bellum. Notable

such depredations by voicing public opinion, the Society for the Preservation of Old Dwellings was organized and began its invaluable work. To it was in large part due· the preservation of the Heyward House on Church Street, threatened at that time by a collector who was picking up houses with the same discrimination as a boy would collect birds' eggs. This society, with co-operation of the Charleston Museum and a number of public-spirited people within and without the city, was able to put the Heyward House into the hands of the Museum.

About the same time a very thorough zoning ordinance was prepared, formulating plans not only for saving what was worthwhile from Charleston's past, but giving certain broad rulings for the city's future growth. This ordinance has since been often invoked and has been instrumental in saving not only individual houses but entire neighborhoods from careless, selfish, and unintelligent changes.

The Depression ended house collecting as a hobby; so like the Confederate War, it came to curse and remained, in part, to bless. Several of the most notable and ancient slums, that had festered rather than grown on badly filled creek beds, were ended at this time in recovery projects. Of these, one of the most typical lay just to the west of the old jail. A sizable creek running out of this region from the Ashley was navigable to the corner of Beaufain and Smith Streets as late as the 1840's. Soon thereafter what is properly Rutledge Street Pond, if offi-

College of Charleston
66 George Street
Nationally Important as a group with Library and Lodge. Central portion by Strickland in 1828, portico and wings by E. B. White in 1850

College of Charleston Library
66 George Street, 1854-56

College of Charleston Lodge
66 George Street. 1852

74 George Street
Ante Bellum. Notable

10, 12 Gillon Street
Post Revolutionary. Notable

6 Gibbes Street
Parker-Drayton House
c. 1806. Valuable to City

6 Glebe Street
St. Philip's Parish Glebe House
c. 1770. Valuable to City

7 Gibbes Street
1804-11. Notable

Mt. Zion A.M.E. Methodist Church
7 Glebe Street
1847. Valuable to City

cially Colonial Lake, was formed into a basin for planters' boats. The marshes above the pond were then filled for building, how unsuccessfully you can estimate by a glance at the would-be vertical in many a good house thereupon. These also formed a respectable front for a slum covering the old creek head and embodying nearly everything bad about this city, until Mills Manor with its good planning and substantial building took its place.

What are Charleston's next steps? Of two things, thinking citizens are more than assured. The harbor, always Charleston's main reason for existence, has been used in this war as never before; today it has upon it such facilities for handling freight and ships as are found nowhere else between Norfolk and Rio de Janeiro. These facilities exist so far from that part of Charleston that most excites the interest of tourists that they can not possibly interfere. Next to the harbor as an asset, and of late positively more valuable, is Charleston's visible history. The tourist business of necessity has been suspended by the War. After the War, more than ever, the American tourists will have to travel in their own country. But even without such stimulation, Charleston has in this business a legitimate industry that it would be the rankest folly to cripple or destroy. Best of all, she needs no copyright or patent to protect it from without. The Village of Williamsburg could be resurrected but at the cost of millions. The City of Charleston can be preserved at the cost of

6, 4, Green Street
Ante Bellum. Notable
No. 6 Relocated

10, 8 Green Street
Ante Bellum. Notable
No. 8 **GONE**
No. 10 Restored

14 Green Street
Ante Bellum. Notable

4 Greenhill Street
Samuel Axson House
Between 1806 and 1813. Notable

37 Hasell Street
c. 1840
Valuable

West End of Grove Street
Lowndes House. Valuable
Before 1790
Piazzas c. 1830

41 Hasell Street
Ante Bellum. Notable

Building formerly used by
congregation of St. John's
Episcopal Church.
16 Hanover Street
Ante Bellum. Notable

St. Johannes Lutheran Church
48 Hasell Street
1842. Valuable to City

only a little continuous intelligent precaution.

And besides, most Charlestonians would like to keep Charleston much as she is for her own sake and theirs. The town is worthy of it. Certain problems with regard to some buildings are doubtless hard to meet; but, by and large, what is good in the city's architecture is good in itself and of itself. Until new structural materials are developed, or more substantial ones are applied to domestic use, people simply cannot build today the sort of house that old Charleston has kept for us. For everything from the virgin timber of the mud sills to the bronze tacks that hold on the slates is either unobtainable or hard and expensive to get. So a sound old house, whatever its age, is an asset to begin with, or to build upon.

The problem of preservation is largely one of appreciation. You get from a thing interest on what you bring to it. On the other hand, a study of what you have at hand is a direct help to good life, and the Charlestonian who neglects his opportunities to see and know and understand his own city renounces a birthright unsurpassed on this side of the Atlantic.

SAMUEL GAILLARD STONEY, 1944

EDITOR'S NOTE. *Based on information available in 1944, Stoney, on page 23, identifies the Col. William Rhett House, 54 Hasell St., built before 1716, as the oldest traceable building in the city. Research completed in 1975 by Elias Ball Bull indicates the Lining House, 106 Broad St., was built c. 1694. If this is correct, the Lining House is the oldest house in Charleston.*

50 Hasell Street
Ante Bellum. Notable
c. 1843

Remodeled as a group in the 1940's, Nos. 54-62 Hasell Street and their accessories, have been made vastly more valuable to the city and the community.

54 Hasell Street
Col. William Rhett House
c. 1712. Nationally Important

58

62, 60 Hasell Street
c. 1847. Valuable to City

64 Hasell Street
Ante Bellum. Notable

60, 58 Hasell Street
c. 1847. Valuable to City

86 Hasell Street
c. 1797. Notable

55 Hasell Street
Ante Bellum. Notable

Beth Elohim Synagogue
90 Hasell Street
1840. Valuable to City

St. Mary's Roman Catholic Church
89 Hasell Street
1840. Valuable to City

29 John Street
Old South Carolina Railway Building
Ante Bellum. Notable

4 John Street
Post Revolutionary. Notable

South Carolina Railway Warehouse
42 Mary Street
Ante Bellum. Notable

14 John Street
Ante Bellum. Notable
GONE

10 Judith Street
Post Revolutionary. Valuable

8 King Street
Notable

22 King Street
Notable
c. 1789

19 King Street
Pre-Revolutionary. Notable

23 King Street
Notable

21 King Street
Notable. c. 1851

24 King Street
Notable
Balcony once on 56 Broad Street

27 King Street, Miles Brewton House
c. 1769. Nationally Important

46 King Street
c. 1851. Notable

41 King Street
Pre-Revolutionary. Valuable

52-50 King Street
Pre-Revolutionary. Valuable

44 King Street
Ante Bellum. Notable
Before 1796

54 King Street
c. 1768. Valuable

55 King Street, Charles Fraser House
1762. Valuable to City

77 King Street
Ante Bellum. Notable
Altered

73 King Street
c. 1820. Valuable
Improved

These substantial houses (Nos. 75, 77, 79,
81, 84, 94, 96 and 98) came back into respectable demand in the 1930's after a long
career as slums.

75 King Street.
c. 1739. Notable

79 King Street
Notable
c. 1747

81 King Street
Notable

114 King Street
c. 1768. Notable
Fine building, if mutilated

84 King Street
Notable

121 King Street
Post Revolutionary. Notable
GONE

98, 96, 94 King Street
Valuable for themselves and as a group
c. 1742

134 King Street
Post Revolutionary. Notable
GONE

134 King Street, kitchen building **GONE**

186 King Street
Valuable. Once one of the most interesting
store fronts in Charleston. Altered

205 King Street
Ante Bellum. Notable
GONE

213 King Street
Ante Bellum. Notable
Very interesting construction
GONE

219, 217 King Street
Ante Bellum. Notable

270 King Street
1872. Notable
ALTERED

299 King Street
c. 1843. Notable
GONE

313 King Street, parking lot
Notable new work

313 King Street
Post Revolutionary. Valuable
A valuable old building adapted
to contemporary use

St. Matthew's Lutheran Church
405 King Street
1867-72. Valuable to City

313 King Street, parking lot
GONE

409 King Street
Ante Bellum. Notable
"The Rev. Ferdinand Jacobs Seminary
for Girls"

66

456 King Street, Aiken House
c. 1811. Valuable to City

30, 28 Lamboll Street
Post Revolutionary. Valuable

456 King Street, Aiken House

48 Laurens Street
Post Revolutionary. Valuable to City

456 King Street, carriage house
Valuable to City. Domestic Gothic

53 Laurens Street
Ante Bellum. Valuable

55 Laurens Street
1818, Valuable

14 Legare Street
c. 1800. Nationally Important
Francis Simmons House
George Edwards Gateway

57 Laurens Street
c. 1836. Valuable
Typical of the 1830's

15 Legare Street
c. 1772. Valuable

8 Legare Street
Ante Bellum. c. 1857
House Notable. Gateway Valuable

16 Legare Street
c. 1795. Valuable
A dignified house with fine interiors

18 Legare Street
Valuable

23 Legare Street, Gate
Notable

21 Legare Street
c. 1843. Valuable
Note masking windows

29 Legare Street
Notable
c. 1835

22 Legare Street
c. 1764. Valuable

31 Legare Street
c. 1789. Valuable to City

32 Legare Street
Valuable to City. Gates
(c. 1848) of same design as the
grilles once in the Greek Doric
Guardhouse at the corner of
Broad Street and Meeting Street.
This premises is also valuable for
fine garden and house
Garden **GONE**

9 Liberty Street
Pre-Revolutionary. Valuable
GONE

122 Logan Street
Notable
Altered

39 Legare Street
c. 1852. **Notable**

1 Lucas Street (now 69 Barre)
Gov. Thomas Bennett House
c. 1822. Valuable to City

Old County Jail, 21 Magazine Street
Ante Bellum. Valuable to City

Old Citadel, Interior of Quadrangle

1, 3, 5, Maiden Lane
Ante Bellum. Valuable as a
picturesque and harmonious group
1 and 3 GONE

44 Mary Street
Ante Bellum. Notable
Interesting masked piazza

Old Citadel, Marion Square
1829-32. Story added c. 1910
Valuable to City

1 Meeting Street
Between 1846 and 1850. Notable

7 Meeting Street, Josiah Smith House
Before 1788. Valuable to City

15 Meeting Street, John Edwards House
c. 1770. Valuable to City

8 Meeting Street, Ladson House
Valuable to City

18 Meeting Street
Thomas Heyward House
c. 1806. Valuable to City

12 Meeting Street
Notable

25 Meeting Street
c. 1760. Valuable

26 Meeting Street
William Mason Smith House
c. 1822. Valuable to City

30 Meeting Street
c. 1769. Valuable

31 Meeting Street
Notable. A very notable garden
Ante Bellum

27 Meeting Street
Post Revolutionary. Valuable
Cast iron gates, recent

34 Meeting Street
Daniel Elliott Huger House
c. 1760. Nationally Important
Famous for its fine interiors

73

36 Meeting Street
Valuable
A Pre-Revolutionary house well altered

47 Meeting Street
Ante Bellum. Notable
Piazzas removed

37 Meeting Street
Pre-Revolutionary. Notable

51 Meeting Street
Nathaniel Russell House
c. 1809. Nationally Important
Now headquarters of Historic
Charleston Foundation

43 Meeting Street
Notable

54 Meeting Street
c. 1800
Valuable though extensively remodeled

74

First Scotch Presbyterian Church
57 Meeting Street
1814. Valuable to City

59 Meeting Street
Branford-Horry House
c. 1751. Nationally Important
Piazzas from 1830

64 Meeting Street
Andrew Hasell 1788-89
House

69 Meeting Street, carriage house **GONE**

69 Meeting Street
Notable. Adam house with Victorian
carriage house

South Carolina Society Hall
72 Meeting Street
Nationally Important
Gabriel Manigault's building, 1804
Frederick Wesner's portico, 1825

76 Meeting Street, Elihu Hall Bay
House. 1785. Valuable

St. Michael's Episcopal Church
80 Meeting Street
1751-61. Nationally Important

Court House, 77 Meeting Street
1752-88. Nationally Important
Provincial State House altered
many times.

Fireproof Building, 100 Meeting Street
1822. Nationally Important
The old Record Offices now used by
the South Carolina Historical Society
Robert Mills, architect

76

Hibernian Society Hall
105 Meeting Street
1840. Valuable to City

Circular Congregational Church
Parish House, 138 Meeting Street
Lance Hall
Valuable to City

St. John Hotel, 115 Meeting Street
1853. Valuable
GONE—Rebuilt 1970

141 Meeting Street
1876. Valuable

Circular Congregational Church
150 Meeting Street
1890. Valuable
Richardson Romanesque

Market Hall, 188 Meeting Street
1841. Valuable to City

271 Meeting Street
Alexander Shirras House
Before 1811. Valuable to City
GONE

Charleston Hotel, 200 Meeting Street
1839. Valuable to City. High tide
of Charleston railroad commerce
GONE

251 Meeting Street
Valuable. Lost by alterations

271 Meeting Street, rear view
Accessory buildings
GONE

78

Trinity Methodist Church
275 Meeting Street
1850. Valuable to City
Formerly Westminster Presbyterian

281 Meeting Street
GONE

278 Meeting Street
Notable

281 Meeting Street, carriage house
GONE

281 Meeting Street
Post Revolutionary. Valuable to City
Notable Adam house with handsome
accessory buildings
GONE

282 Meeting Street
Notable
GONE

285 Meeting Street
Post Revolutionary
Notable despite butchery
GONE

289 Meeting Street
1870. Notable

296 Meeting Street
Valuable. The Adam period in little

286 Meeting Street
Post Revolutionary. Valuable to City
Once a handsome Adam house
Altered c. 1807

Citadel Square Baptist Church
328 Meeting Street
1856. Valuable to City

Second Presbyterian Church
342 Meeting Street
1811. Valuable to City

Joseph Manigault House, Lodge

Second Presbyterian Church

379 Meeting Street
Ante Bellum. Notable
GONE

Joseph Manigault House
350 Meeting Street
c. 1802. Nationally Important
Owned by the Charleston Museum
Gabriel Manigault, architect

392 Meeting Street
Valuable
One of the few half timbered houses
in Charleston
GONE

416 Meeting Street
Ante Bellum. Notable
GONE

18 Montague Street
House of Benjamin Smith of
Goose Creek, excellent interiors
c. 1788. Valuable

31 Mill Street
Notable

20 Montague Street
Dr. James Moultrie House
Post Revolutionary. Valuable

11, 13 Montague Street
Ante Bellum. Notable
No. 11 has particularly charming
doorway

28 Montague Street
Notable. Old house, somewhat
modern piazzas

82

54 Montague Street
Ante Bellum. Valuable

64 Montague Street
Before 1814. Notable. Portico
originally over stair landing
later extended into piazzas

60 Montague Street
Gaillard-Bennett House
c. 1800. Valuable to City

37 New Street
Ante Bellum. Notable

62 Montague Street
Ante Bellum. Notable

4 Orange Street
Valuable to City
Unspoiled Pre-Revolutionary interiors

7 Orange Street
c. 1769. Valuable
Built by Col. Charles Pinckney

9 Orange Street
c. 1770. Valuable to City
Pre-Revolutionary two family house

11 Orange Street
Home of Samuel and Caroline Gilman
c. 1770. Valuable to City

8 Orange Street
c. 1770. Valuable to City
Small Pre-Revolutionary house with
modern addition

13 Pitt Street
Ante Bellum. Notable
c. 1859

84

36 Pitt Street
Ante Bellum. Notable
Altered

83 Pitt Street
Ante Bellum. Notable
GONE

56 Pitt Street
Ante Bellum. Notable

1 Prioleau Street
Ante Bellum. Valuable

Bethel Methodist Church
57 Pitt Street
1853. Valuable to City

5 Prioleau Street, Old Cotton Exchange
Ante Bellum. Notable
GONE

5 Queen Street
Ante Bellum. Valuable
Very interesting brick work on
a commercial building

10, 8 Queen Street
Ante Bellum. Notable

18, 16, 14 Queen Street
Notable

6 Queen Street
Ante Bellum. Notable
Improved

19 Queen Street
Valuable
GONE

20 Queen Street
Ante Bellum. Notable
Charleston in a West Indian aspect

23, 25 Queen Street
Post Revolutionary. Notable

28, 26, 24, 22 Queen Street
Post Revolutionary. Valuable to City

28, 26, 24, 22 Queen Street
View of roofs

30 Queen Street
Post Revolutionary. Valuable

44 Queen Street
c. 1800. Notable
A notable cartouche on balcony

46 Queen Street, accessory buildings
c. 1800. Valuable to City

45 Queen Street
Pre-Revolutionary. Valuable
GONE

Cathedral School, 105 Queen Street
After Fire of 1861. Notable
Once the Pro-Cathedral
GONE

45 Queen Street, servants' quarters
Improved since 1944

Gateway of Orphan Home
120 Queen Street
Ante Bellum. Notable
GONE

88

127, 129 Queen Street
Ante Bellum. No. 127 Notable
A notable example of the Charleston
single house

160, 162 Queen Street, rear view

153, 155 Queen Street
Ante Bellum. Notable

165 Queen Street
Notable

162, 160 Queen Street
Ante Bellum. Valuable

192 Queen Street
c. 1850. Notable

47 Radcliffe Street
Ante Bellum. Notable
GONE

74 Rutledge Avenue
c. 1800. Valuable for house and
fine old garden

57 Radcliffe Street, also known as
25 Thomas Street
c. 1816. Valuable
A West Indian type house dating from
the time when this was country

81 Rutledge Avenue
Ante Bellum. Notable

67 Rutledge Avenue
Notable

93 Rutledge Avenue
Ante Bellum. Valuable

90

94 Rutledge Avenue
1853. Valuable to City
I. Jenkins Mikell House, Sea Island
cotton planter's Charleston residence

140 Rutledge Avenue
Ante Bellum. Notable
GONE

94 Rutledge Avenue, kitchen building
IMPROVED

145 Rutledge Avenue
Ante Bellum. Notable **GONE**

95 Rutledge Avenue
Ante Bellum
Notable for its interiors

156 Rutledge Avenue
Post Revolutionary. Valuable. Home of
William Johnson, the historian and
Justice of the United States
Supreme Court. c. 1808

160 Rutledge Avenue
Ante Bellum. Notable
A fine house with a fine garden
GONE

179 Rutledge Avenue
Between 1874 and 1886. Notable
A perfect Victorian in Charleston guise

Ashley Hall School
172 Rutledge School
c. 1816. Valuable to City
Patrick Duncan House

185 Rutledge Avenue
Post Revolutionary. Notable
Note extremely interesting cornice

173 Rutledge Avenue
Ante Bellum. Valuable
GONE

8 St. Michael's Alley
Office of James L. Petigru
1848. Valuable

6 St. Philip Street
Ante Bellum. Notable
Masked piazza on an interesting
small house
GONE

101 St. Philip Street
1829 and 1850. Notable in spite of
unfortunate treatments
GONE

50 St. Philip Street
"Miss Kelly's School"
Notable
GONE

34 Smith Street
Ante Bellum. Notable
c. 1855

56 St. Philip Street
Post Revolutionary. Valuable
Plantation type house
GONE

47, 49 Smith Street
Ante Bellum. Notable

48 Smith Street
Ante Bellum. Notable in spite of
losses from alterations

54 Smith Street
Ante Bellum. Notable

51 Smith Street
Ante Bellum. Notable
Altered

59 Smith Street
Ante Bellum. Valuable

52 Smith Street
Ante Bellum. Notable

63 Smith Street
Ante Bellum. Notable

67 Smith Street
Post Revolutionary. Notable

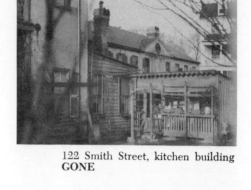

122 Smith Street, kitchen building
GONE

89 Smith Street
Ante Bellum. Valuable

46 Society Street
Ante Bellum. Notable
Improved

122 Smith Street
Post Revolutionary. Notable
GONE

55 Society Street
Old High School Building
c. 1840. Portico 1850
Valuable to City
Improved

64 Society Street
Ante Bellum. Notable

8 South Battery
Gen. William Washington House
c. 1768. Nationally Important

66 Society Street
Ante Bellum. Notable

32 South Battery
Col. John Ashe House
c. 1782. Valuable

4 South Battery, Villa Margherita
Modern. Notable
Chicago Exposition style in Charleston

39 South Battery, Moreland House
c. 1827. Valuable to City
Second piazza is an old
alteration

44 South Battery
Ante Bellum. Notable

58 South Battery, John Blake House
Post Revolutionary. Valuable

48 South Battery
c. 1846. Valuable
Excellent Greek Revival in the
Charleston tradition

64 South Battery
1772-89. Nationally Important
Gibbes House, Roebling garden

56 South Battery
Post Revolutionary. Valuable
A picturesque house devoid of
pretentiousness

68 South Battery
1797-1843. Valuable to City
A handsome house with beautiful
new garden

Spring Street Methodist Church
68 Spring Street
1858. Valuable to City

11 State Street
Post Revolutionary. Notable

12 State Street
Ante Bellum. Valuable. A fine
example of a Charleston single house
Improved

7 State Street
Old Fire Insurance Company
Post Revolutionary. Valuable

13 State Street
Post Revolutionary. Valuable

24, 22 State Street
Post Revolutionary. Notable

25 State Street
c. 1814. Notable
Entrance Altered

27 State Street
c. 1813. Valuable to City
A picturesque and functional
use of a small premises

27½ State Street
c. 1813. Valuable to City
Improved

38, 36 State Street
Post Revolutionary. Valuable

42 State Street
c. 1816. Notable
Improved

7 Stoll's Alley
Pre-Revolutionary. Notable. Probably
very early house, doorway modern

13 Thomas Street
Post Revolutionary. Notable

9 Stoll's Alley
Pre-Revolutionary. Valuable
Doorway modern

St. Mark's Episcopal Church
14 Thomas Street
Before 1887. Notable

6 Thomas Street
James Legaré House
Also known as the Robert Barnwell Rhett
House. c. 1832. Valuable to City

15 Thomas Street
Ante Bellum. Valuable

25 Thomas Street
(See 57 Radcliffe St.)

East End of Tradd Street
(South Adger's Wharf)
Ante Bellum. Valuable
Improved

East End of Tradd Street
(South Adger's Wharf)
Ante Bellum. Notable

5, 7 Tradd Street
Pre Revolutionary. Notable
c. 1727

1 Tradd Street
c. 1785. Notable

6 Tradd Street
Before 1789. Notable

101

10, 8 Tradd Street
c. 1726 Notable

15 Tradd Street
Pre-Revolutionary. Valuable

11, 13 Tradd Street
c. 1781. Notable
NO. 11 **GONE**

17 Tradd Street
Post-Revolutionary. Notable

16, 14, 12 Tradd Street and
2 Bedon's Alley
c. 1778. Notable

19 Tradd Street
Pre-Revolutionary. Notable
c. 1747

19, 23, 25 Tradd Street
Post-Revolutionary. Notable

32 Tradd Street
Post-Revolutionary. Notable

35 Tradd Street
Pre-Revolutionary. Valuable

28, 26 Tradd Street
Post Revolutionary. Notable

44, 40, 38 Tradd Street
Pre-Revolutionary. Notable
No. 38, 40. c. 1718

41, 43 Tradd Street
Pre-Revolutionary. Valuable
c. 1746

51, 53 Tradd Street
c. 1736. Notable
Improved

46 Tradd Street
c. 1770. Valuable

49 Tradd Street
Pre-Revolutionary. Valuable to City

54 Tradd Street
Postmaser Bacot House
c. 1740. Valuable to City

58, 56 Tradd Street
Pre-Revolutionary. Valuable to City

64 Tradd Street
Pre-Revolutionary. Valuable
Entrance altered

61 Tradd Street
c. 1736. Notable

65 Tradd Street
Pre-Revolutionary. Notable

62, 60 Tradd Street
Valuable

70 Tradd Street
Judge Robert Pringle House
1774. Valuable to City

72 Tradd Street
Pre-Revolutionary. Valuable
Improved

92 Tradd Street
Ante Bellum. Notable

80, 78 Tradd Street
Ante Bellum. Notable

101, 103 Tradd Street
Pre-Revolutionary
No. 101 Notable. No. 103 Mention
No. 103 is 1797

75 Tradd Street
Ante Bellum. Valuable

102 Tradd Street
Pre-Revolutionary, Notable

106

106 Tradd Street
Col. John Stuart House
c. 1772. Nationally Important

107 Tradd Street
Valuable. Notable servants' quarters
No. 107 **GONE**

123 Tradd Street
c. 1800. Valuable

125 Tradd Street
c. 1807. Valuable

126 Tradd Street
Mrs. Peter Fayssoux House
c. 1732. Notable

128 Tradd Street
Humphrey Sommers House
c. 1765. Valuable to City

129 Tradd Street
Joseph Winthrop House
c. 1797. Valuable

172 Tradd Street
John Ashe Alston House
Before 1855. Valuable

131 Tradd Street, Gate
Mrs. Ruth Lowndes Simmons House
c. 1804. Notable

Chisolm's Rice Mill, West End
of Tradd Street. 1830. Valuable

143 Tradd Street
Ante Bellum. Notable

8 Vanderhorst Street
Ante Bellum. Notable

108

Charleston Orphan House Chapel
13 Vanderhorst Street
1802. Nationally Important
Designed by Gabriel Manigault
GONE

64 Vanderhorst Street
After 1824. Valuable

61 Vanderhorst Street
Ante Bellum. Notable
GONE

Vendue Range, North Side
Ante Bellum. Notable
Improved

61 Vanderhorst Street, summerhouse
GONE

Vendue Range, South Side
Ante Bellum. Notable

64 Warren Street
Ante Bellum. Notable
Plantation type house

2 Water Street
c. 1812. Notable
Mansard after 1865

86 Warren Street
Ante Bellum. Valuable

14 Water Street
(See 45 Church St.)

89 Warren Street
Chancellor Dunkin House
1823-29. Valuable

Bennett's Rice Mill
East End of Wentworth Street
1844. Nationally Important
Mill architecture as an art
Only West Facade Remains

19 Wentworth Street, cast iron fence
Ante Bellum. Notable

46 Wentworth Street
Ante Bellum. Notable.

St. Andrew's Lutheran Church
43 Wentworth Street
Rebuilt 1838. Valuable

59 Wentworth Street
Notable. Gothic variation on the
Charleston house, once accessory
building to German Artillery Hall
GONE

44 Wentworth Street
Ante Bellum. Notable
GONE

Centenary Methodist Church
60 Wentworth Street
1842. Valuable to City
Built by white Baptists, acquired
by A. M. E. church in 1866

89 Wentworth Street
Post-Revolutionary. Valuable
Fine double house, half modernized

138 Wentworth Street
Charles Kerrison House
c. 1842. Valuable to City

Grace Episcopal Church
100 Wentworth Street
1847. Valuable to City

138 Wentworth Street, bathhouse

111 Wentworth Street
Notable
GONE

144 Wentworth Street
Post-Revolutionary. Valuable to City
Fine interiors

149 Wentworth Street, Rodgers Mansion
Valuable

169 Wentworth Street
Ante Bellum. Notable
Altered

150 Wentworth Street
Ante Bellum. Valuable. Also known as
45 Smith Street. Residence of
Christopher Gustavus Memminger,
Secretary of the Treasury, C. S. A.
GONE

Aiken's Row, Wragg Mall
Ante Bellum. Notable
Partly GONE
Two remain

166 Wentworth Street
Ante Bellum. Notable
c. 1809

Aiken's Row, Wragg Mall
Ante Bellum. Notable
Largely GONE
Two Remain

BUILDINGS CLASSIFIED 1941

BUILDINGS CONSIDERED NATIONALLY IMPORTANT

Broad Street—80
Bull Street—18
Church Street—61, 69, 71, 87, 146
East Bay—122
Franklin Street—20
George Street—66
Hasell Street—54
King Street—27

Legare Street—14
Meeting Street—34, 51, 59, 72, 77, 80, 100, 350
South Battery—8, 64
Tradd Street—106
Vanderhorst Street—13
Wentworth Street—Bennett's Rice Mill, east end of street

BUILDINGS CONSIDERED VALUABLE TO CITY

Anson Street—67
Archdale Street—6, 10, 19
Ashley Avenue—167, 218
Beaufain Street—71, 89
Broad Street—16, 92, 106, 110, 122
Calhoun Street—160, West Point Mill, west end of street
Charlotte Street—16, 20
Church Street—35, 37, 39, 59, 60, 83, 85, 86, 89, 90, 91, 92, 94, 135, 136, 143, 145, 154
Coming Street—126
Court House Square—2, 4
Cumberland Street—21
East Battery—21, 39
East Bay—43, 51, 89, 95, 101, 329
Elizabeth Street—22
George Street—14
Gibbes Street—6
Glebe Street—6, 7
Hasell Street—48, 58, 60, 62, 74, 79
King Street—55, 405, 456

Laurens Street—48
Legare Street—31, 32
Lucas Street—1
Magazine Street—21
Marion Square—Old Citadel
Meeting Street—7, 8, 15, 18, 26, 57, 105, 138, 188, 200, 271, 275, 281, 286, 328, 342
Montague Street—60
Orange Street—4, 8, 9, 11
Pitt Street—57
Queen Street—22, 24, 26, 28, 46
Rutledge Avenue—94, 172
Society Street—55
South Battery—39, 68
Spring Street—68
State Street—27, 27½
Thomas Street—6
Tradd Street—49, 54, 56, 58, 70, 128
Vanderhorst Street—62
Wentworth Street—60, 100, 138, 144

BUILDINGS CONSIDERED VALUABLE

Amherst Street—2
Anson Street—71, 75, 79
Archdale Street—21, 23
Ashley Avenue—61, 109, 113, 178

Atlantic Street—1, 3, 8
Bay Street—Cooper View Apts. at Amherst and Bay Sts.
Bedon's Alley—5

Bee Street—32
Broad Street—1, 33, 35, 49, 50, 60,
    64, 68, 85, 87, 88, 114
Bull Street—48
Calhoun Street—85, 207, 222, 274,
    286
Cannon Street—135
Chalmers Street—17
Chapel Street—28
Charlotte Street—32
Church Street—19, 20, 77, 116, 131
East Battery—9, 13
East Bay—47, 53, 55, 57, 78, 83, 97,
    103, 114, 116, 118, 120, 139, 141,
    178, 200, 217, 301, 321, 332, 333,
    344
Elizabeth Street—7, 48
Elliott Street—20
George Street—21, 28, 36
Grove Street—west end of street
Hanover Street—16
Hasell Street—37
Judith Street—10
King Street—41, 50, 52, 54, 73, 94,
    96, 98, 186, 313
Lamboll Street—28, 30
Laurens Street—53, 55, 57

Legare Street—15, 16, 18, 21, 22
Liberty Street—9
Maiden Lane—1, 3, 5
Meeting Street—25, 27, 30, 36, 54,
    76, 115, 141, 150, 251, 296, 392
Montague Street—18, 20, 54
Orange Street—7
Prioleau Street—1
Queen Street—5, 19, 30, 45, 160,
    162
Radcliffe Street—57
Rutledge Avenue—74, 93, 156, 173
St. Michael's Alley—8
St. Philip Street—56
Smith Street—34, 59, 89
South Battery—32, 48, 56, 58
State Street—7, 12, 13, 38, 40
Stoll's Alley—9
Thomas Street—15, 25
Tradd Street—east end of street, 15,
    35, 41, 43, 46, 60, 62, 64, 72, 75,
    107, 123, 125, 129, 172, Chisolm's
    Rice Mill, west end of street
Vanderhorst Street—64
Warren Street—86, 89
Wentworth Street—43, 89, 149, 150

BUILDINGS CONSIDERED NOTABLE

Ann Street—Camden Depot, 40
Anson Street—30, 114, 116
Archdale Street—38, 41
Ashley Avenue—70, 75, 76, 96, 139,
    163, 192, 217
Bay Street—at Blake Street
Beaufain Street—56, 63, 65, 91, 102,
    108
Broad Street—6, 8, 10, 12, 14, 15,
    28, 54, 67, 93, 95, 100, 102, 105,
    116, 119, 180
Bull Street—96, 99, 100, 104, 112,
    128
Calhoun Street—123, 139, 141, 214,
    220, 261, 268
Cannon Street—134
Chalmers Street—6, 8, 29, 36

Chapel Street—34, 36
Charlotte Street—Gas Works, east
    end of street, 29, 33, 36, 40, 43, 44
Church Street—12, 22, 24, 38, 45,
    47, 55, 75, 76, 78, 79, 100, 102,
    103, 121, 122, 124, 128, 134, cor-
    ner of Church and Hayne Sts.
Coming Street—10, 69, 102, 106,
    110
Cordes Street—entire block
Court House Square—8
Drake Street—105
East Battery—1, 40
East Bay—45, 71, 85, 87, 90, 91, 93,
    107, 131, 137, 154, 162, 188, 190,
    192
Elizabeth Street—19

BUILDINGS CONSIDERED WORTHY OF MENTION

ANALYSIS OF SURVEY 1941

The Survey covered 1380 items. Index cards were made for the total number, including 1168 buildings.

	CARDS MADE
Dwellings	930
Churches	36
Public Buildings	42
Commercial and Industrial	160
Scenic	40
Parks, etc.	13
Cemeteries	19
Gardens	140
	1380

Ratings of Buildings Listed, complete total 1168

	NATIONALLY IMPORTANT	VALUABLE TO CITY	VALUABLE	NOTABLE	MENTION
Dwellings	14	77	136	253	450
Churches	4	21	5	2	4
Public Buildings	7	13	7	11	4
Commercial and Industrial	1	2	21	51	85
Totals	26	113	169	317	543

Age of Buildings

	PRE-REV.	POST-REV.	ANTE-BELLUM	MODERN	UNDATED
Dwellings	71	134	467	44	214
Churches	1	5	23	6	1
Public Buildings		8	25	2	7
Commercial and Industrial	1	19	108	2	30
Totals	73	166	623	54	252

ANALYSIS OF SURVEY (Continued)

Geographic Distribution of Buildings Listed

	OLD AND HISTORIC AREA AND SOUTH OF BROAD	BOROUGHS BETWEEN CALHOUN AND BROAD	NORTH OF CALHOUN
Dwellings	369	407	154
Churches	5	19	12
Public Buildings	18	22	2
Commercial and Industrial	1	130	29
Parks and Cemeteries	7	15	10
Gardens	110	19	11
Totals	510	612	218

Geographic Analysis of Buildings

Old and Historic Area and South of Broad Street

		NATIONALLY IMPORTANT	VALUABLE TO CITY	VALUABLE	NOTABLE	MENTION
Dwellings	369	11	46	74	109	129
Churches	5	3	2			
Public Buildings	18	6	7		5	
Com. and Ind.	1		1			
Gardens	110					
Parks	2					
Cemeteries	5					
Total	510					
Vistas Listed	20					

ANALYSIS OF SURVEY (Continued)

Boroughs Between Broad and Calhoun Streets

		NATIONALLY IMPORTANT	VALUABLE TO CITY	VALUABLE	NOTABLE	MENTION
Dwellings	407	2	27	41	107	230
Churches	19		13	3	1	2
Public Buildings	22	1	5	7	6	3
Com. and Ind.	130	1	1	18	39	71
Gardens	19					
Parks	5					
Cemeteries	10					
Total	612					
Vistas Listed	17					

Boroughs Between Calhoun and Boundary

Dwellings	154	1	4	21	37	91
Churches	12	1	6	2	1	2
Public Buildings	2		1			1
Com. and Ind.	29			3	12	14
Gardens	11					
Parks	6					
Cemeteries	4					
Total	218					
Vistas Listed	3					

Use of Buildings Listed in Survey

Dwellings, total   930
     Single, 490
     Multiple, 440
Commercial Buildings with Dwelling Units   67 (1)
Religious   36 (2)
Educational   1
Philanthropic   2

ANALYSIS OF SURVEY (Continued)

Use of Buildings Listed in Survey (Continued)

Social	8 (3)
Commercial and Industrial	160
Social and Commercial	2 (4)
Social and Educational	6
Governmental	6
Public Buildings for Miscellaneous Use	15
Abandoned	2

These figures apply to present uses, not uses for which the buildings were designed. Many commercial buildings (1), for instance, were intended originally to be purely dwellings, and some combined the two uses. These buildings are listed as dwellings on the foregoing tables. One building designed for religious use (2) has been made a recreation center for a housing project. (3) includes buildings like the South Carolina Hall and the Hibernian Hall which were built and are maintained by organizations. (4) includes buildings of organizations which included shops.

The base map on which the following charts and diagrams were superimposed was drawn in April, 1944. All streets were arbitrarily widened to admit street names.

WHITE POINT WITH ITS CREEKS AND MARSHES

Information taken from map in *Charleston Year Book, 1884*, Mesne-Conveyance Records, McCrady maps in the R.M.C. Office, and map compiled by the Charleston Museum.

123

THE "GRAND MODELL"
WITH CERTAIN EARLY PLANTATION LINES

A Platt of Charles-Town

The original "grand modell" or city plan was made between 1670-80, probably before 1673. It was lost or destroyed, but copies existed. The copy owned by the South Carolina Historical Society was preserved by Gen. W. G. DeSaussure from among papers marked for destruction at the City Hall. It is accompanied by a list of landowners which is dated 1725, and entitled: "The Numbers, Grants, and their Dates, Title Page where entered of the Several Books, &c of the Town Lots of Land in Charles Town." A copy of the platt of 1725 was made by the Hon. Henry A. M. Smith for the *South Carolina Historical and Genealogical Magazine*, Vol. IX.

Information taken from map compiled from notes by Gen. W. G. DeSaussure, now in possession of the Charleston Library Society and *The Dwelling Houses of Charleston* by Alice R. Huger Smith and D. E. Huger Smith.

HARLESTON

Part of the grant made to John Coming (whose widow was the donor of the Glebe Lands) in 1685. After the death of John Coming and his wife, it was inherited by Mrs. Coming's nephews, the Harlestons, whose name the section bore when it was developed and streets were opened up in 1770. The streets were patriotically named for famous men of the day.

GLEBE LANDS

Seventeen acres given to the minister of the Church of England in Charles Town and his successors in office forever, by Mrs. Affra Coming, 1698. Land divided into 38 building lots in 1770, and into 14 more lots created, and Glebe Street cut through in 1797.

RMCO V7-5

MAZYCK LANDS

Land granted to James Moore in 1698, conveyed by trustees of his will, 1712, to Isaac Mazyck. In 1742 partitioned among the four sons of Isaac Mazyck and others.

RMCO B3-460

RMCO B3-486

Plat Book, City Engineer's Office, p. 58.

FREE SCHOOL LANDS

Land given in 1710 by Act of Assembly (A/a yol. 11, 389, 342) for a Free School, and later (D vol. IV, 675) 1785, reserved for the use of the College of Charleston.

RHETTSBURY

Land granted to William Rhett in 1714 and known as Point Plantation of Rhettsbury. Divided by his great-grand-daughters, Susannah and Mary Hasell, whose marriages to Parker Quince and John Ancrum were formerly commemorated in the streets of Rhettsbury.

RMCO LH6-491
McCrady Plats, Case 45

GEN. CHRISTOPHER GADSDEN'S LANDS OR MIDDLESEX

An original grant to Isaac Mazyck in 1720. After successive owners, 20 acres of high land and 20 acres of marsh were sold to Gadsden, who had them divided into six wharf lots and 197 back lots, built a brick market, and with Alexander Mazyck, his neighbor, provided a canal and landing. He named the streets for his political interests, but most of them have been changed.

RMCO 13-313, Q5-251
Plat Book CEO, p. 40.

ANSONBOROUGH

In 1726, George Anson, then captain of a naval patrol based here, got this land. In the War of Jenkin's Ear he fought his way to fame and fortune, becoming later a baron and Admiral of the Fleet. Ansonborough, developed in 1747, got for its streets his names, and those of ships he had commanded; the Squirrel and Scarborough, here; the Centurion, on which he rounded the world raiding Spain's colonies and commerce. Since 1959 this has been the site of the Historic Charleston Foundation's Ansonborough Rehabilitation Project.

WRAGG LANDS AND WRAGG PASTURE LANDS

Parts of the grant to Joseph Wragg, partitioned among his son John and others in 1751. The lower portion was the allotment of Henrietta Wragg. The upper was penetrated by a marshy creek that extended to Pitt Street.

RMCO B3-247

WRAGGBOROUGH

Land that was a part of the extensive holdings of Joseph Wragg, partitioned among John Wragg and others in 1751. John Wragg received the 79 acres on the east of the "Broad Path" (King Street). A plat of 1806 shows it substantially as it exists today. The streets of Wraggboro were named with the Christian names of the Wragg children. The two parks were created in 1801.

RMCO B3-247, A7-415
Plat Book, CEO p. 24

CANNONSBORO

A low and marshy tract owned between 1762 and 1800 by Daniel Cannon, a house carpenter and mechanic, who owned lumber mills here. (Plat Book, CEO p. 80.) A plat made for the division of lots belonging to the heirs of Jonathan Lucas in 1853 shows a large part of this same area.

MAZYCKBOROUGH

Land developed by Alexander Mazyck. Surveyed "at the request of the proprietor" and streets laid off by J. Purcell, 1786.

RMCO L3-414
Plat Book, CEO p. 144.

RADCLIFFEBORO AND ELLIOTT LANDS

The former (lower section) was developed by Thomas Radcliffe, and surveyed by J. Purcell, 1786.

RMCO, McCrady Plats, Bk. 2, p. 38

Elliott Lands on Charleston Neck were also surveyed by J. Purcell in 1786.

HAMPSTEAD

Laid out for Henry Laurens in 1789.

RMCO Y10-45
Plat Book, CEO p. 8

FORTIFICATIONS
AND MARSH LINES

Information taken from map in *Charleston Year Book, 1884.*

FIRE AREAS

Information taken from map compiled by the
Charleston Museum.

133

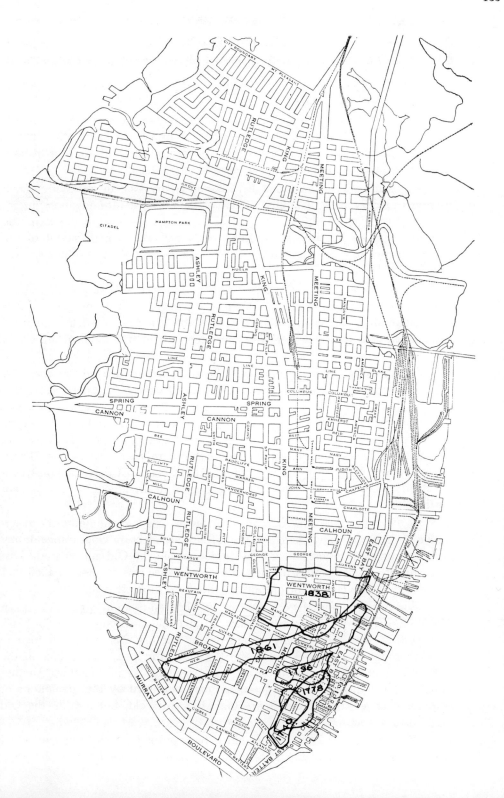

THE ZONING ORDINANCE

Charleston's Zoning Ordinance, adopted in 1931, attracted national attention because of a section protecting historic and esthetic values. The ordinance was based on a survey made that same year of the physical and economic aspects of the city and its buildings. The new ordinance provided, among other things, for an "Old and Historic Area" in which "historic places and areas of historic interest" would be preserved and protected.

The measure was commended by Charles Henry Cheney of California, a pioneer in modern city planning, as "one of the most forward advances in city planning work and architectural control that we have ever had yet in the country," and by Dr. Robert D. Kohn of New York, then president of the American Institute of Architects, as "the most progressive ordinance ever adopted in America."

Today more than 200 American cities have followed the lead of Charleston and have enacted some sort of ordinance to preserve private property of historic or architectural value. Many, perhaps the majority, of such ordinances have relied heavily on the original Charleston law for both nomenclature and substance.

The Charleston zoning ordinance was and is administered by the City Planning and Zoning Commission and the City Engineer. A Board of Adjustment has authority to interpret the Ordinance and grant variances. A Board of Architectural Review has under its special protection the "Old and Historic Districts" of the city. This Board now consists of seven members, five of whom represent professional groups and two of whom are appointed by the Mayor. A requirement for the Mayor's appointees is that they must "have demonstrated outstanding interest and knowledge in historical or architectural development of the city."

Since 1931, the Board of Architectural Review has had the authority to approve or disapprove any change in the exterior architectural appearance of any structure or any proposed new construction within the Old and Historic District. But it was not until a revision of the ordinance was enacted in 1966 that the Board was given specific authority actually to prohibit demolition.

The original Old and Historic District was limited to an area of 138 acres in the southeast corner of the city almost all of it below Broad Street. In 1966, the District was substantially enlarged—by another 290 acres—to include Ansonborough, the Mazyck lands and the Harleston area, and to take in the fine old commercial streets of Broad and some blocks of Meeting. Another amendment to the original law gave the Board authority to delay demolition or exterior changes to buildings more than 100 years old, but outside the Old and Historic Districts.

In 1971, the City of Charleston, aided by a grant from the Department of Archives and History of the State of South Carolina, commissioned the prep-

Old and Historic
District as of 1975

aration of a "Historic Preservation Plan". The report was delivered in 1974 and was the culminaton of three years of research and study by professional consultants with the assistance of many of Charleston's citizens and organizations. It included an inventory of architecture south of the Cross-town Expressway within the peninsular city. In 1975, City Council amended the zoning law to make this the official inventory of the city. The amendment also instructed the Board of Architectural Review to be guided by the inventory in approving applications for demolition or alteration of buildings under its jurisdiction.

Also in 1975, City Council again enlarged the Old and Historic District to include nearly all of the peninsular city below Calhoun Street, plus part of the historic neighborhoods of Radcliffeborough, Wraggborough and Mazyckborough, above Calhoun Street. This added another 361 acres to the District, and brought the total to 789 acres, and includes substantial portions of the center city commercial district.

Meanwhile, the effectiveness of the City Planning and Zoning Commission had been increased. This occurred with the establishment in 1974 of the City Department of Planning, Relocation and Redevelopment, with a full-time director and staff of planners and technicians The old fire station at Meeting and Queen Streets is now being renovated to provide office space, including a hearing room, for this department, as well as the City Engineer and others concerned with administering the zoning and building inspection laws.

DISTRIBUTIONS
OF BUILDINGS
INCLUDED IN
THE SURVEY

ADDENDUM

The four houses pictured below were not included in the original edition of *This is Charleston*. The editors of this 1976 edition believe that the houses should have been included, and therefore they are herewith presented as an addendum.

43 Legare St. Built
c. 1759 by Charles Elliott.

9 Limehouse St.
William Pinckney Shingler's first house,
c. 1856.

7 Limehouse St.
Robert Limehouse House,
c. 1830

10 Limehouse St.
William Pinckney Shingler's
second house, c. 1858.